One hop
FORWARD. ⬆

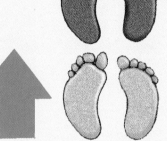

One hop
BACKWARD. ⬇

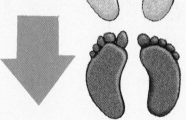

Repeat four times
and you'll be
right back where
you started.
Then sing:
"Wiggle left.
Wiggle right.
Do the bug dance
every night!"

turn
RIGHT! ➡

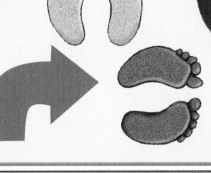

BUG DANCE

MathStart® DIRECTIONS

by Stuart J. Murphy

illustrated by Christopher Santoro

HarperCollins Publishers

LEVEL
1

To Jane—whose dancing eyes make everyone smile—S.J.M.

To Nathan and Jim, who are always a step or two ahead—C.S.

The publisher and author would like to thank teachers Patricia Chase, Phyllis Goldman, and Patrick Hopfensperger for their help in making the math in MathStart just right for kids.

HarperCollins®, 📚®, and MathStart® are registered trademarks of HarperCollins Publishers.
For more information about the MathStart series, write to
HarperCollins Children's Books, 1350 Avenue of the Americas, New York, NY 10019,
or visit our website at www.mathstartbooks.com.

Bugs incorporated in the MathStart series design were painted by Jon Buller.

Library of Congress Cataloging-in-Publication Data

Murphy, Stuart J.
    Bug dance / by Stuart J. Murphy / illustrated by Christopher Santoro.
       p.   cm.– (MathStart)
"Level 1."
ISBN 0-06-028910-4 – ISBN 0-06-028911-2 (lib. bdg.) – ISBN 0-06-446252-8 (pbk.)
    1. Orientation–Juvenile literature.   [1. Orientation.]   I. Santoro, Christopher, ill.   II. Title.
III. Series.
QP443.M8   2002   00-044867
513.2'11–dc21

Typography by Elynn Cohen 1 2 3 4 5 6 7 8 9 10 ❖ First Edition

All the bugs loved gym class, especially Centipede. He loved dodgeball. He loved freeze tag. He loved jumping jacks. Centipede couldn't wait to find out what they would be doing today.

Coach Caterpillar announced, "Today we're going to try a dance."

"Dance!" said Centipede. "I can't dance. I always trip over all my feet!"

"Maybe this time will be different," said his friend Cricket. "You're kidding," said Inchworm. "Centipedes aren't made to dance. They're not like inchworms. We're very graceful."

"First I'll show you the dance," Coach Caterpillar explained. "Then we can all do it together."

She turned around so she was facing the same way as the class. And she sang,

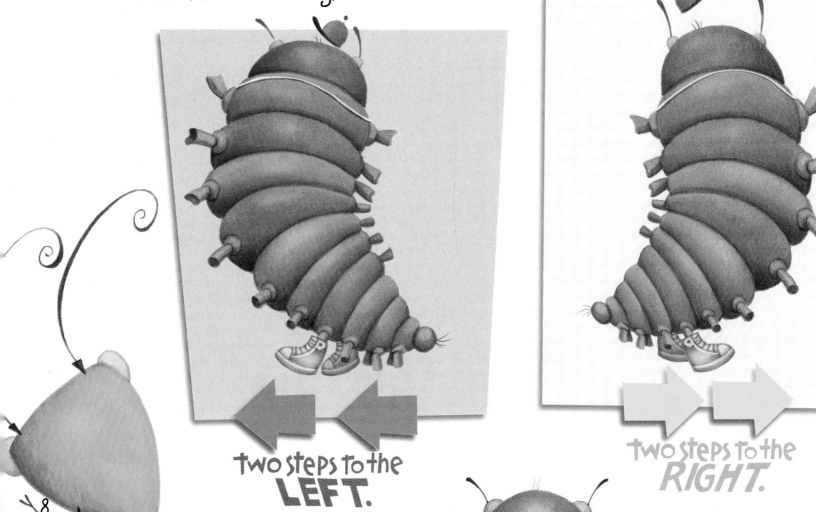

two steps to the
LEFT.

two steps to the
RIGHT.

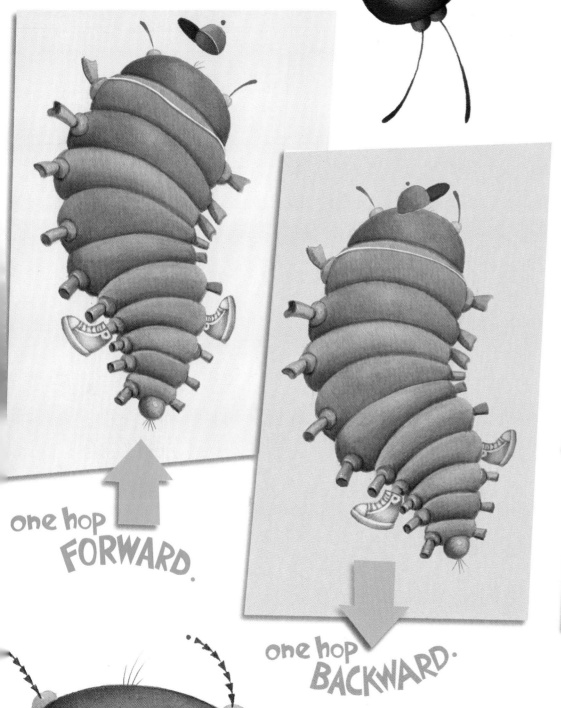
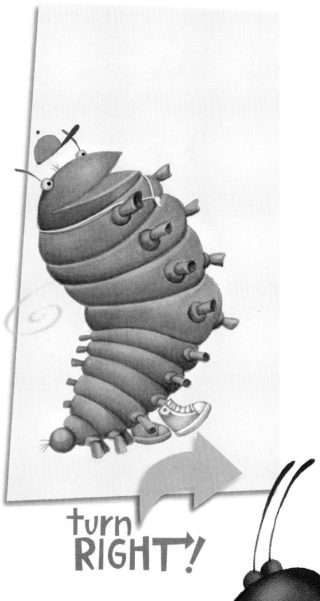

one hop
FORWARD.

one hop
BACKWARD.

turn
RIGHT!

"Wow! That looks great," said Cricket.

"I can't wait to try it," said Fly.

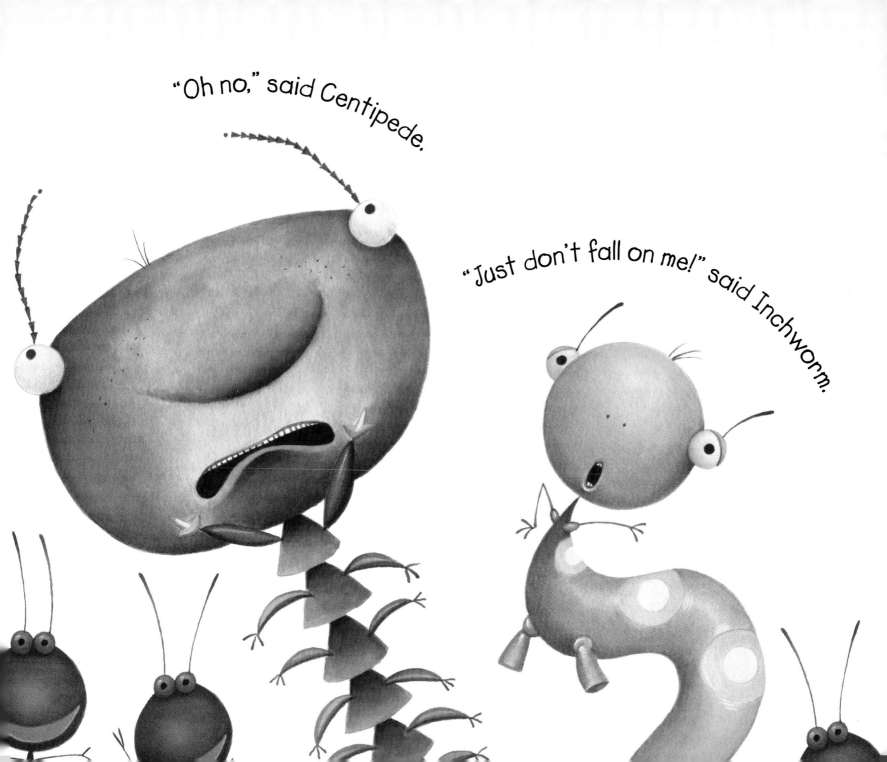

Coach Caterpillar repeated the steps three times. When she finished, she was right back where she started. Then she called out, "Now everybody follow me!"

two steps to the **LEFT.**

two steps to the... **FLOP!**

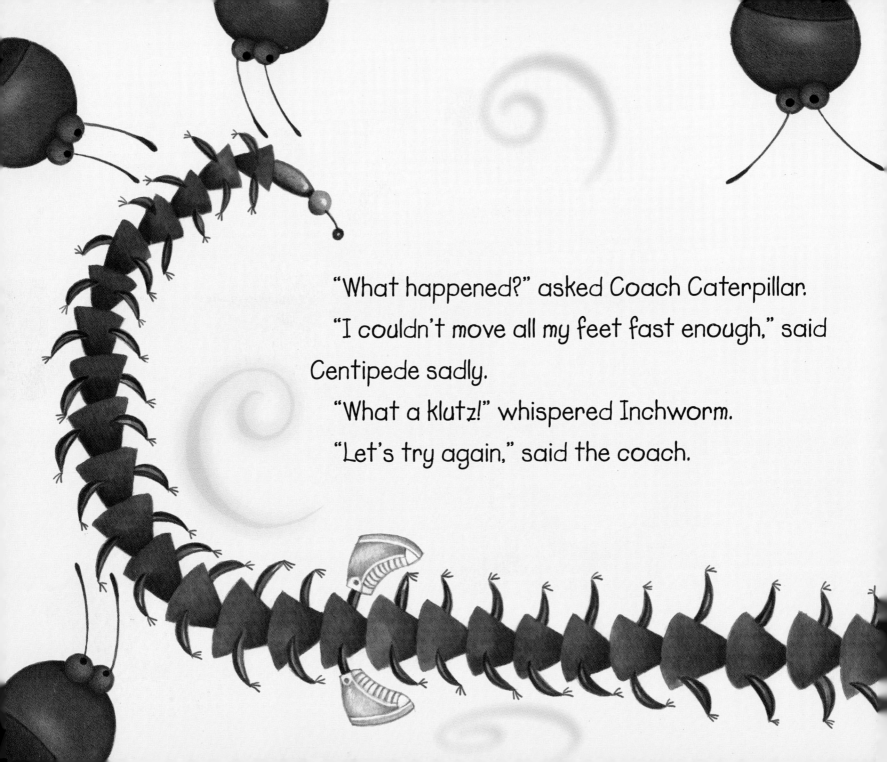

"What happened?" asked Coach Caterpillar.

"I couldn't move all my feet fast enough," said Centipede sadly.

"What a klutz!" whispered Inchworm.

"Let's try again," said the coach.

"Ready . . . set . . . start!" yelled Coach Caterpillar.

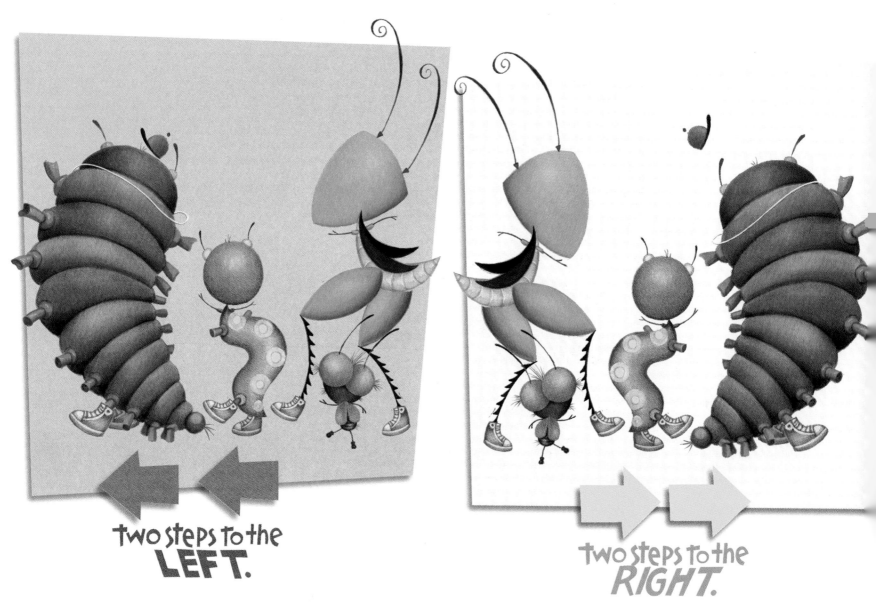

two steps to the
LEFT.

two steps to the
RIGHT.

16

one hop FORWARD...

wHOOPS!

18

"Is everybody okay?" asked Coach Caterpillar.
"Centipede got stuck again," said Cricket.
"I *almost* had it," said Centipede.
"No way!" said Inchworm.

"Okay, one more time," said the coach.

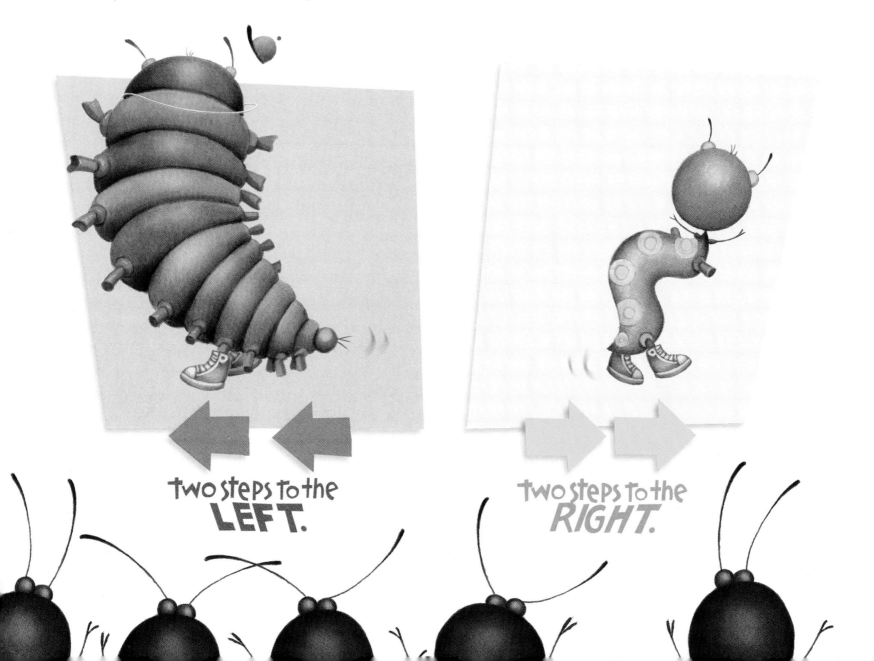

two steps to the
LEFT.

two steps to the
RIGHT.

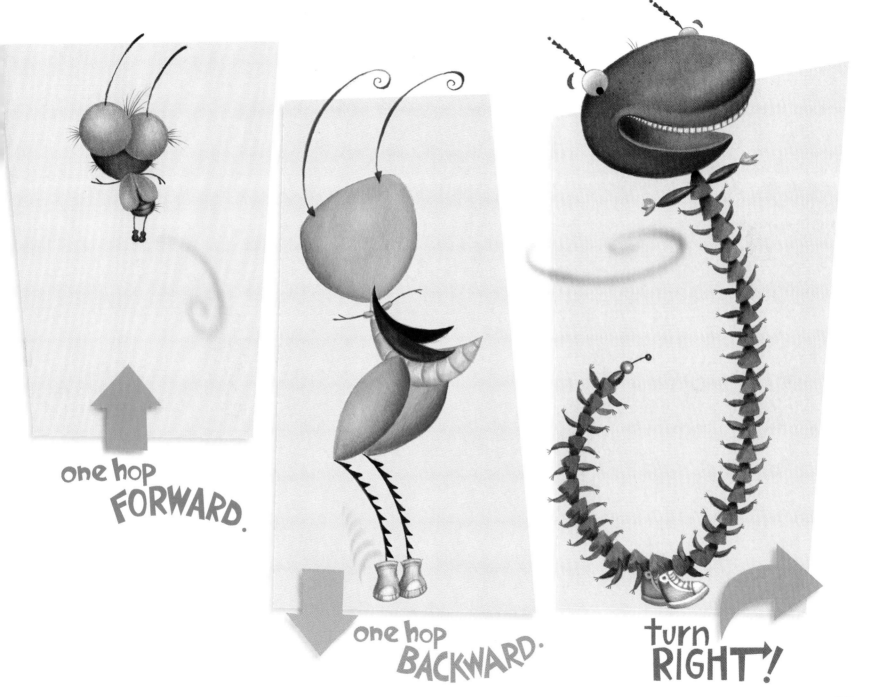

one hop
FORWARD.

one hop
BACKWARD.

turn
RIGHT?!

21

"You're doing great, Centipede," said Cricket.

"We've got it now," said Fly.

"This is fun!" said Centipede.

"But you have to do it *three more times*," said Inchworm. "You'll never make it."

But they did the dance three more times. They ended up right where they started.

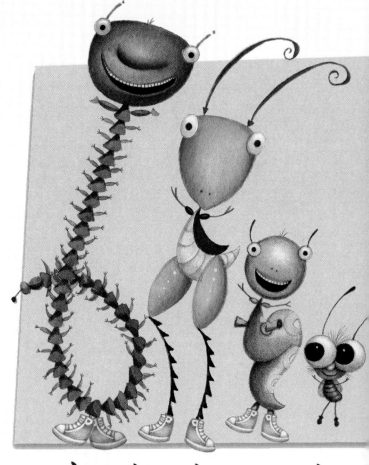

And Centipede didn't trip once.

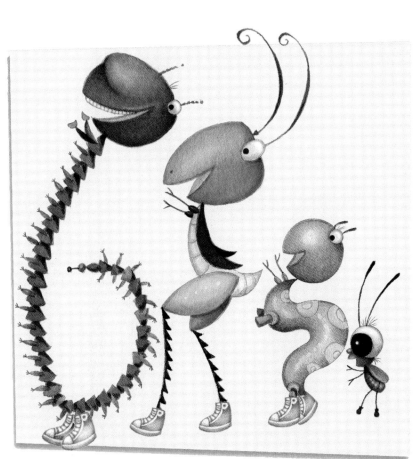
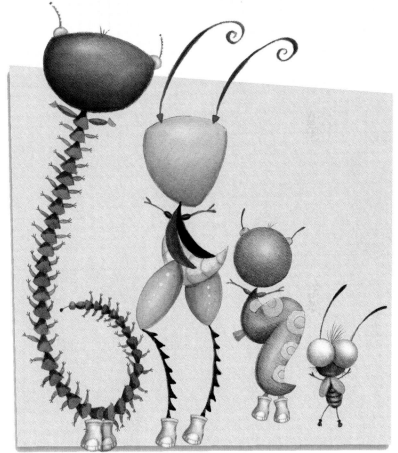

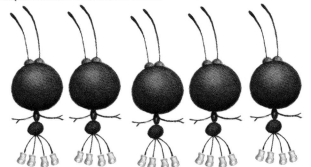

"Great job!" said the coach. "Now I'll teach you the ending." Coach Caterpillar turned around and asked, "Ready?" Then she sang,

"Wiggle LEFT.
Wiggle RIGHT.
Do the bug dance every night!"

"Well," said Inchworm. "I guess centipedes can dance after all. But they're not as good as inchworms. Watch this!"

Inchworm did a little spin. She did a little jig. And she jumped into the air . . .

27

. . . a little too high.

PLOP!

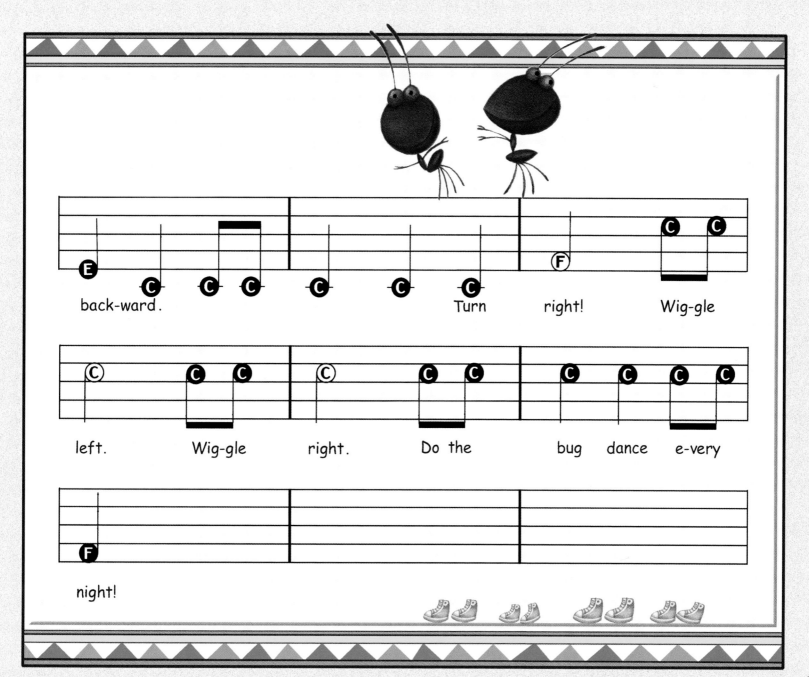

In *Bug Dance* the math concept is direction—*right, left, backward,* and *forward.* Knowing these 4 basic directions lays a foundation for map skills and geometry.

If you would like to have more fun with the math concepts presented in *Bug Dance,* here are a few suggestions:

- Have the child wiggle his or her left and right hands, and then left and right feet. Face the same direction as the child and have him or her identify your left and right hands and feet. To help the child remember, you can place a string or a loose rubber band on his or her right hand. You could also point out that the thumb and first finger on the left hand form the letter *L.*

- Read the story to the child and discuss which direction the bugs are moving.

- Read the book a second time and have the child pretend to be the centipede and follow the dance directions.

- Sing "The Hokey Pokey" and have the child follow the directions in the song.

- Copy the diagrams below and have the child trace them without lifting his or her crayon, describing the directions the crayon is moving.

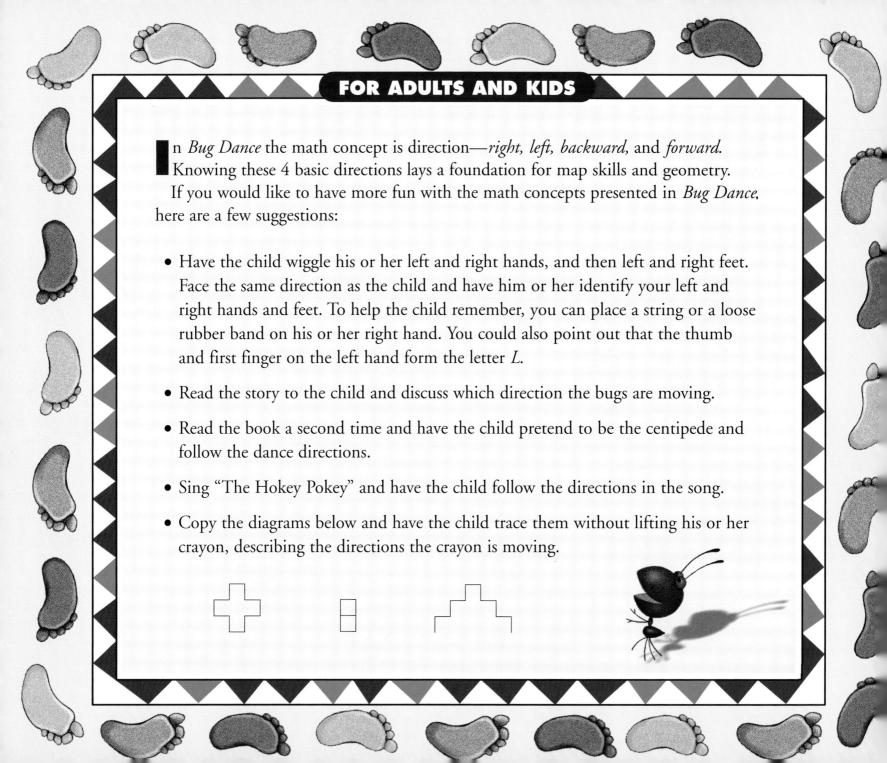

Following are some activities that will help you extend the concepts presented in *Bug Dance* into a child's everyday life:

Dance: Have the child use his or her favorite song and create a dance using directions similar to the ones in the story. Have the child record the steps and then teach the dance to other members of the family.

Planning a Walk: Plan a walk to a park or store. Draw a simple map of the route you will follow and have the child help with the directions. After the directions are written out, follow the directions and take the walk.

Game: Play the game Simon Says with the child. Give directions such as "Make one big jump forward" or "Take two steps to your left." If you preface the directions with "Simon says," the child should follow them; if not, he or she should remain still. If the child makes a move for which you did not say "Simon says," he or she sits out the next turn.

The following books include some of the same concepts that are presented in *Bug Dance*:

- REX'S DANCE by Fay Robinson

- DANCE AWAY by George Shannon

- WHICH WAY, BEN BUNNY? by Mavis Smith